# Achieving Consensus

*Tools and Techniques*

## Jon Scott

## Eileen Flanigan

## *A Crisp Fifty-Minute*™ *Series Book*

This Fifty-Minute™ book is designed to be "read with a pencil." It is an excellent workbook for self-study as well as classroom learning. All material is copyright-protected and cannot be duplicated without permission from the publisher. *Therefore, be sure to order a copy for every training participant by contacting:*

THOMSON
NETg

1-800-442-7477 • 25 Thomson Place, Boston MA • www.courseilt.com

# Achieving Consensus

*Tools and Techniques*

**Jon Scott**
**Eileen Flanigan**

## CREDITS:

Product Manager: **Debbie Woodbury**
Production Editor: **Genevieve McDermott**
Managing Editor: **Kathleen Barcos**
Editor: **Kay Keppler**
Production Artists: **Nicole Phillips, Rich Lehl, and Betty Hopkins**
Manufacturing: **Stephanie Porreca**

**ISBN** 1-56052-381-6
Library of Congress Catalog Card Number 2003115570
Printed in the United States
09 10 11 12  09 08 07 06

# Learning Objectives For:

## ACHIEVING CONSENSUS

The objectives for *Achieving Consensus* are listed below. They have been developed to guide the user to the core issues covered in this book.

### THE OBJECTIVES OF THIS BOOK ARE TO HELP THE USER:

1) Understand the definition of consensus

2) Explore individual roles on the road to consensus

3) Learn the steps needed to create consensus

4) Gain problem-solving tools and techniques

### ASSESSING PROGRESS

NETg has developed a Crisp Series **assessment** that covers the fundamental information presented in this book. A 25-item, multiple-choice and true/false questionnaire allows the reader to evaluate his or her comprehension of the subject matter. To download the assessment and answer key, go to www.courseilt.com and search on the book title, or call 1-800-442-7477.

*Assessments should not be used in any employee selection process.*

# ABOUT THE AUTHORS

**JON SCOTT,** MBA, MS in systems management, has experience in business, technology and education, specializing in corporate change, process improvement, team building and facilitation.

Since the early 1980s, Jon has focused primarily on becoming a change agent in the improvement of operations deemed critical by company leadership. These real-world, hands-on experiences have developed his practical approach to unleashing people's potential in the workplace.

**EILEEN FLANIGAN,** MBA, is a consultant, meeting facilitator and corporate trainer specializing in team dynamics, facilitation and process change.

For the past 10 years Eileen has facilitated groups to bring about positive organizational change. She has been using successful consensus building as a key to facilitating change, as well as inspiring others to use this tool.

Eileen teaches and works with companies as diverse as Volkswagen USA, Novell, and Hughes Aircraft.

# CONTENTS

# INTRODUCTION

*Achieving Consensus* looks at consensus as a process—a process that brings different people, different ideas and different approaches together; values that diversity, and then provides a framework to create a solution that is greater than any one person, idea or approach. It is the opportunity to set aside the "I" for the success of the "we." It is the opportunity to get the power of the group aligned to get things done.

Information on teaming and facilitation has addressed consensus briefly, discussing its definition, pitfalls, and the role of the facilitator. While this information is helpful, it doesn't address how to get consensus to work in the real world. Pressures that must be recognized and are addressed in this book include assessing and improving your skill set; dealing with deadlines; getting the group going; and using tools to overcome behavior and decision obstacles. These components include:

► Participants' skills

► The need to grow into new skills

► Using boundaries to frame issues

► Tools for addressing behavioral and decision obstacles

As the world shifts focus from individual achievement to group success, skills to accomplish this shift must be learned. The paradox is that to achieve group success, each of us as individuals must be able to contribute to the group and help it reach consensus. Achieving consensus is as much about an individual journey as it is about the journey of the group.

This book explores both the individual and group journey and provides readers with the tools necessary to add value to their next team or group assignment and to have some fun while doing it.

# P A R T

## *I*

# Defining Consensus

## *Planning Checklist*

☑ **Choose Your Destination**

☐ Decide What to Pack

☐ Understand Your Traveling Companions

☐ Select Your Route

☐ Prepare to Tackle Any Roadblock or Obstacle

# WHAT IS CONSENSUS?

*"Success is turning knowledge into positive action."*
—Dorothy Leeds

*Achieving consensus* is a *journey* that *begins with multiple points of view* and *ends with mutual agreement.* You can say that you have reached consensus when you can answer yes to the following:

▶ The agreement (or decision or solution or plan) meets or exceeds your needs

▶ The agreement meets or exceeds the other group members' individual needs

▶ The agreement addresses the reason the group first got together

▶ Everyone in the group will work to support the agreement

If you can agree to these points, then you have reached consensus. If you cannot answer to yes to these points, then you and your group have more work to do before you can say that you have reached consensus. Getting to yes is not an easy task, but once there you'll be amazed at the energy you have to make things happen and get things done.

> **Idea:** Consensus gets the power of the group aligned to get things done.

# CONSENSUS AS A PROCESS

Reaching consensus is about the journey that begins with "I" and ends in "we." When defined as a process, reaching consensus is very straight-forward. It looks like this.

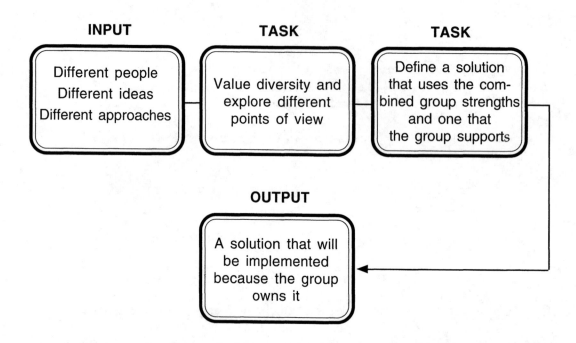

**INPUT**

Different people
Different ideas
Different approaches

**TASK**

Value diversity and explore different points of view

**TASK**

Define a solution that uses the combined group strengths and one that the group supports

**OUTPUT**

A solution that will be implemented because the group owns it

**Idea:** If you own something, you take better care of it. Consensus creates a feeling of ownership.

# REACHING CONSENSUS IS LIKE TAKING A JOURNEY

Journeys must be organized and planned. How do you keep track of everything you have to do? You make a list.

## Choose Your Destination

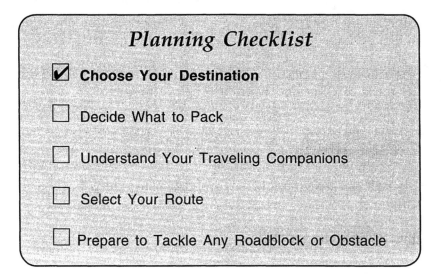

*Planning Checklist*

☑ **Choose Your Destination**

☐ Decide What to Pack

☐ Understand Your Traveling Companions

☐ Select Your Route

☐ Prepare to Tackle Any Roadblock or Obstacle

We will be taking a journey to a mythical place called Consensusville—a place where decisions are made by consensus. If you were boarding a plane, this would be the point where the flight attendant said: "Please check your tickets. This plane is going to Consensusville. If that is not your desired destination, then please signal the nearest flight attendant."

**Idea:** Working to consensus requires personal risk, but the rewards are usually worth it.

# SELECTING CONSENSUSVILLE

Consensusville is a much talked about, but often elusive destination. The trip is planned because the news is out about the great things accomplished by the residents of Consensusville. Who knows, you may even decide to move to Consensusville after experiencing what the travel guide calls that "small town feeling of trust and achievement—a town where people roll up their sleeves and pitch in to make it a better place. It's a place where you can help make things happen."

Even though some people think that Consensusville is a great place, one shouldn't be too hasty in selecting a destination. Before choosing Consensusville, perhaps you should check out some alternatives.

Are you ready to make a personal change that can increase the chances that you will get more of what you want and help others too?

## Other Destinations

Some people will say that the journey to Consensusville is not worth it. They might say that:

- It takes too long to get there

- The route to get there is too complicated

- You might not like it once you arrive

They might recommend a trip to places like Votesburg or BossTown. Before going too far on the journey, let's make sure you're going to the right place. Let's compare the decision styles of "working to consensus" (Consensusville) to "majority rule" (Votesburg) and "unilateral decision maker" (BossTown).

Before you go on, think of a past group situation that you would classify as a positive experience.

*What things made it a positive experience?* _____

_____

*What lessons did you learn from that experience?* _____

_____

Think of a past group situation that you would classify as a negative experience.

*What things made it a negative experience?* _____

_____

*What lessons did you learn from that experience?* _____

_____

As you go on, think of the positive and negative experience and how the decision-making styles used in those situations influenced your perceptions.

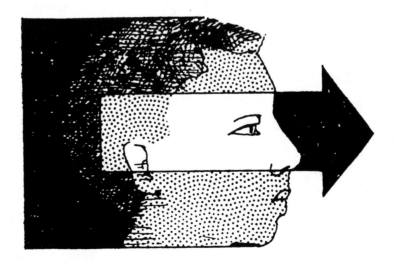

# HOW CONSENSUS FITS WITH OTHER DECISION STYLES

There are many ways to reach a decision other than consensus. Two of the most common styles are:

- Majority rule (Votesburg)

- One person decides unilaterally or with input from the group (BossTown)

These styles have three things in common.

**1.** Both of these styles get to a decision faster than working to consensus.

**2.** Both of these styles are less complex than using consensus and therefore easier to explain and use.

**3.** Both of these styles allow some members of the group to avoid individual responsibility for the decision.

## Majority Rule (Votesburg)

Many political systems are based on majority rule. After all, it is impractical to get millions of people to come to consensus. It is difficult enough to get people to care enough to come out to vote. Why is this? Perhaps people think that their actions will not make a difference. The result is voter indifference. Do you vote in every election? Do you stay current on events and let your representatives know what you want? If not, why not? Most of the citizens of Votesburg do not understand why things get decided, but then don't get done.

*What percentage of your experience has been with this style?* _____

_____

*How did you feel about the results?* _____

_____

# Unilateral Decision Making (BossTown)

Many businesses are based on the dictatorship approach, which assumes that most people in the business do not have access to all the information they need to make a decision. Somebody must decide and usually must decide quickly (because little planning was done). Usually that somebody is the boss. Perhaps the boss consults the group, perhaps not, depending on the situation's urgency and whether it is easy to get feedback. Either way the boss makes the decision. After the boss decides, the citizens of BossTown usually feel ignored or angered.

*What percentage of your experience has been with this style?* _____

_____

*How did you feel about the results?* _____

_____

> **Idea:** The trip is quick and easy to Votesburg and BossTown, but the travelers don't help steer.

SIMPLIFIED DECISION MAKING

JUST DO IT!

Sound familiar?

# SOURCES OF DIFFICULTY

If you set Consensusville as your destination, know the issues and temptations that you will face along the way. Here are a few of the potential hurdles.

## Power of the Boss

You may not be able to change how your boss behaves toward you, but you can control how you behave toward those who work for you. Some people, as soon as they are in any position of authority, turn into dictators. The power goes to their head. They love to hear themselves talk and monopolize all conversations.

## Going for the Quick Fix

Many people just want to get things done. Schedule is more important than quality. Working to consensus means resisting the pressure to "just get it over with" and instead working to accomplish something lasting.

## Competing Priorities

There are always more things to do than there are hours in the day. One day one item is important, and the next day something else is important. Getting and staying focused is a major challenge.

## High Rate of Change

If you act too slowly, then everything will keep changing faster than your ability to keep up with it. You will never reach consensus. If you act too quickly, then you may not have true support from the group. A sense of timing is critical.

## Complexities

Most problems are not straightforward. Sometimes it may be easier to ignore those confounding facts that make everything too complicated, but it usually works out that you either address the complexities now or pay double in the future.

## Your Own Emotional State

It takes a lot of trust and self-confidence to disclose what you want and permit the group to arrive at a decision that is in your best interest. If you are upset, it is difficult to participate as part of the group. You must be aware of your emotional state and set the example for others.

*As you understand working to consensus, what is the most difficult thing for you to accept about it?* _____

_____

*Are you willing to keep an open mind?* _____

_____

# EXERCISE: *True/False*

Read the following questions and check either True or False. Check your answers against those in the box at the bottom of the page.

|  | True | False |
|---|:---:|:---:|
| 1. Only the boss must set the example of how to relate to others. | ☐ | ☐ |
| 2. Getting and staying focused is a major challenge. | ☐ | ☐ |
| 3. Most problems are straightforward. | ☐ | ☐ |
| 4. It takes a lot of self-confidence and trust to disclose what you really want. | ☐ | ☐ |
| 5. Meeting schedules is more important than quality. | ☐ | ☐ |
| 6. It is common for power to go to people's head. | ☐ | ☐ |
| 7. Unilateral decision making is the most fulfilling form of making decisions. | ☐ | ☐ |
| 8. Getting to consensus is a slow process. | ☐ | ☐ |

**Answers:** 1. F (you must), 2. T, 3. F, 4. T, 5. F, 6. T (unfortunately), 7. F, 8. T

# YOUR JOURNEY

If you made it this far, then it is safe to assume that you want to know more about how to work to consensus. You have made the decision to take a journey to Consensusville. Your journey is a personal one. It is about you. It is about what you can do, not what others should do. Your journey will help you to think about your actions and what you can change to make yourself more effective, since you cannot control anyone but yourself. Working to consensus requires something more from yourself. If you are willing to give that extra something, then you will receive the benefits associated with helping others get what they want. Congratulations for selecting Consensusville as your destination!

*What do you think that you will have to change about yourself to make consensus work for you?* _____

_____

Now that you have selected your destination, the next step is to decide what to pack to take with you.

# II

# Your Role on the Road to Consensus

## Planning Checklist

- ☐ Choose Your Destination

- ☑ **Decide What to Pack**

- ☐ Understand Your Traveling Companions

- ☐ Select Your Route

- ☐ Prepare to Tackle Any Roadblock or Obstacle

# DECIDING WHAT TO PACK

*"When one is wise, two are happy."*

—Plutarch

What do you need for your journey to Consensusville? We all carry baggage. Sometimes our baggage contains just the perfect things that we need. Sometimes our baggage does nothing but weigh us down. The trick is to take a careful, honest inventory and decide what you need and leave the rest.

## *Planning Checklist*

- ☐ Choose Your Destination

- ☑ **Decide What to Pack**

- ☐ Understand Your Traveling Companions

- ☐ Select Your Route

- ☐ Prepare to Tackle Any Roadblock or Obstacle

# YOUR PERSONAL INVENTORY

Your personal inventory is what you bring to the group. Of course, every other group member has a personal inventory, too. Often members arrive thinking that their inventory is more valuable than anyone else's. The types of things that you have in your personal inventory, to one degree or another, are:

- ► **COMMUNICATION SKILLS**—The ability to share information clearly and accurately and listen to understand another point of view.

- ► **PROBLEM-SOLVING SKILLS**—The ability to break down a problem or issue into its components and offer creative and timely solutions to resolve it.

- ► **EDUCATION**—Knowledge gained through formal classroom time or book study.

- ► **EXPERIENCE**—Knowledge gained through hands-on work.

- ► **POWER BASE**—Strength of position earned by providing recognized leadership, which can be used to gain support.

- ► **PEOPLE SKILLS**—Ability to work effectively with diverse groups of people.

- ► **CONFLICT-MANAGEMENT SKILLS**—Ability to draw on skills that can aid you and others to manage and resolve areas of disagreement.

All participants, including yourself, come to the table with different strengths and blind spots in their personal inventories. The trick is to understand these traits and the power they represent to the rest of the group. One way to do that is to diagram them. The diagrams on page 19 show, by the size of the circles, the personal inventories of two people.

PERSON ONE: Jeff is a group member who has excellent skills in communication and conflict management. Because he is new to the company, he has not yet developed much direct experience or a base of power.

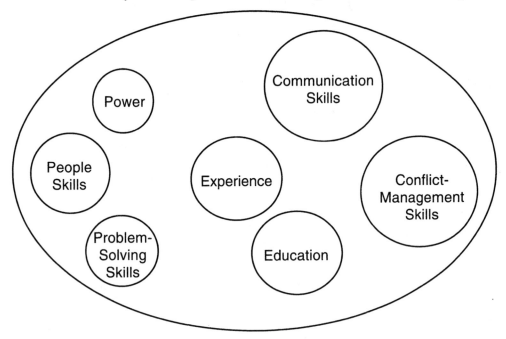

PERSON TWO: Amy is a group member who has an MBA and a power base developed through her leadership as manager of the department. Her direct experience on the topic is limited, and she needs to work on her conflict-management skills.

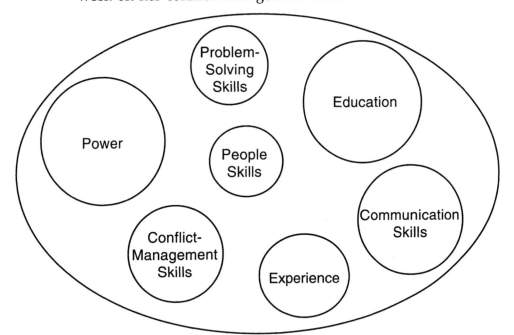

# YOUR PERSONAL INVENTORY (continued)

*How does varying the size of the circles affect the way a person views consensus?* _____

_____

*How does changing the mix of people affect the way a group works toward consensus?* _____

_____

Fill in the blank personal inventory below. What are your strongest areas? Weakest?

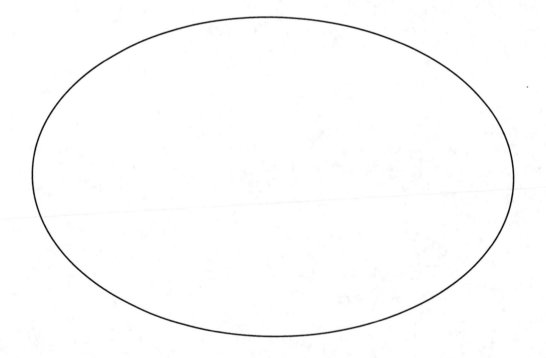

Each person comes to a group with his or her own skill sets. Each person thinks that his or her experience is the most important, so opportunities abound for misunderstanding and conflict. Usually, this initial blending of skills and experiences does not create an environment open to the consensus process. Here is an example.

# CASE STUDY: *The A to Z Corporation*

The A to Z Corporation's product shows low sales. The president has created a team with representatives from all departments to improve this issue. The departments are asked for solutions. Here is a summary of their responses.

- **Information Systems Department:** We need to install a new computer system so we can take orders over the phone.

- **Engineering Department:** We need to redesign the product to make it easier to use.

- **Marketing Department:** We need more money for an ad campaign.

- **Manufacturing Department:** We need to install that new automated production line that would cut our assembly costs so we could reduce the price.

- **Human Resources Department:** We need to train our people so that they can be more effective.

- **Quality Department:** We need to increase our quality levels.

- **Finance Department:** We don't have the money to spend on anything.

*Who was right?* _____

_____

*Why?* _____

_____

_____

_____

# YOUR PERSONAL INVENTORY (continued)

## Case Study Review

*They were all right and all wrong.* Most organizations and people look at things from their perspective. They communicate in the ways they are comfortable with and value the things that are important to them. They argue why they are right. They do not look at things from a different point of view because it is hard enough to understand things from their own point of view. Sometimes it seems that we spend most of our time trying to convince other people that everything would be fine if they would just accept our point of view.

> **Idea:** If we could combine our skills and experiences, think how much we could achieve.

## EXERCISE: *True/False*

Read the following questions and check either True or False. Check your answers against those in the box at the bottom of the page.

|  | True | False |
|---|---|---|
| 1. People often think their skills and knowledge are more valuable than anyone else's. | ☐ | ☐ |
| 2. Each person's strengths and weaknesses are unique to that person. | ☐ | ☐ |
| 3. The initial blending of skills and experience creates an environment open to the consensus process. | ☐ | ☐ |
| 4. Every issue can have many points of view. | ☐ | ☐ |
| 5. There is always one best answer. | ☐ | ☐ |

**Answers:** 1. T, 2. T, 3. F, 4. T, 5. F

# TAKING INVENTORY

Take a personal inventory to recognize what your unique skills and experiences are. The survey that follows will give you some insight into your personal baggage. You might want to fill a survey out on yourself and then ask friends or colleagues to complete one using you as the subject.

## *Personal Inventory*

| After reading each question, rate your skills on a scale of 1–5 with 5 being most proficient. | Needs Work | Getting There | Moderately Proficient | Proficient | Highly Proficient |
|---|---|---|---|---|---|
| I form my thoughts and ideas into words easily and others understand the intent of my message. | 1 | 2 | 3 | 4 | 5 |
| I listen to understand what others are telling me and I repeat back what I hear to verify the message. | 1 | 2 | 3 | 4 | 5 |
| I break down issues or problems into their components before I try to come to a solution. | 1 | 2 | 3 | 4 | 5 |
| I am timely and creative in coming to solutions for problems. | 1 | 2 | 3 | 4 | 5 |
| I have pursued formal education in my chosen area of study. | 1 | 2 | 3 | 4 | 5 |
| I take classes to stay current in an ever-changing environment. | 1 | 2 | 3 | 4 | 5 |
| I stick with an area long enough to gain background knowledge and experience. | 1 | 2 | 3 | 4 | 5 |
| I understand the details of my area of expertise. | 1 | 2 | 3 | 4 | 5 |
| I am a recognized leader and others look to me for that skill. | 1 | 2 | 3 | 4 | 5 |
| I can get things done using my connections with other people. | 1 | 2 | 3 | 4 | 5 |
| I interact easily with people who are different from me. | 1 | 2 | 3 | 4 | 5 |
| I am comfortable participating in conflict situations. | 1 | 2 | 3 | 4 | 5 |
| I help others to see alternate points of view in conflict situations. | 1 | 2 | 3 | 4 | 5 |
| I can separate my own issues to help move toward resolution of conflict. | 1 | 2 | 3 | 4 | 5 |
| Add the scores in each column then across the bottom. The higher your overall score, the more skills you bring to the consensus process. | | | | | |

# UNDERSTANDING OTHER PEOPLE

After you understand yourself and what you bring on the trip, the next step is to understand the people that you are working with in the group. You may not be able to get each one of them to take a personal inventory, but you can learn a lot just by observing them. Keeping in mind the questions in the personal inventory, watch the other people in your group interact and see where their skills lie. Understanding your own and others' strengths and weaknesses helps set reasonable expectations and allows you and the group to work together more effectively.

# THINGS TO LEAVE BEHIND

As you go through your suitcase, you probably will find a few things that you want to leave behind. These items are found in most people's luggage. Do your best to leave behind these four attitudes.

> **I Don't Want to Lose**
>
> **I Resist Change**
>
> **I Am Stuck in a Rut**
>
> **I Love/Hate Conflict**

Let's take a quick look at these items so you can recognize them in your luggage.

## I Don't Want to Lose

When you get caught up in a win-lose proposition, the game becomes achieving what is good just for you—not the group as a whole. This philosophy of win-lose affects your interaction with others, your level of honesty in the discussion and your willingness to listen to another point of view. You are so busy figuring out how to get the group to adopt your position that you cannot work as part of the group. Many aspects of society are based on competition, so it is natural that this attitude would spill over into your own behavior and that of your group members. The best path is to advocate consensus (win-win) up front. If it appears that members of the group are competing (win-lose), get this issue on the table and address it.

## I Resist Change

Resistance is an internal barrier to change. It surfaces when our beliefs or values appear to be threatened. Resistance is often accompanied by physical sensations of tension, anger or a feeling of being overwhelmed. Resistance to change is normal, but you can make a conscious decision to look at your beliefs or values in relation to the topic of discussion without moving into an emotional reaction. There are two things you can do to keep a clear head.

# THINGS TO LEAVE BEHIND (continued)

**1.** Remember that understanding the other person's position does not mean that you have to agree with it. Listen to understand the other point of view and try to understand why that person believes it.

**2.** Be open to the idea that you do not have all the answers to all the questions in the universe. If you admit that there are other possibilities, it will be easier to find them.

## I Am Stuck in a Rut

If you have been working with the same people for some time, they expect to see you act in the way you always have. If you start acting differently, they wonder about you. They will try to get you to act as you always have. If you want to try something different, then you have to act differently. The first place to change things is with yourself. You can change.

> **Idea:** If you can't change yourself, why do you expect everyone else to change?

## I Love/Hate Conflict

Consensus building and good decisions usually find their roots in healthy debate and energetic discussions. A total lack of conflict is one sign of a poorly functioning group. Every smart boss knows the danger of too many "yes" people. The other end of the scale is unmanaged conflict. If there is no managed closure, the one who argues the loudest wins. We have all been in cases where we see the same issues come up time and time again, and we never seem to make any progress. You need to speak your mind, but you need to listen to others, too.

*What is the one piece of baggage that you want to leave behind?* _____

_____

*How would your life change if you left that piece of baggage behind?* _____

_____

# FOCUS ON STRENGTHS, NOT WEAKNESSES

Even though you would like to leave some things behind, probably you will not get rid of all your unwanted baggage at one time. Therefore, it is important to create an environment where you and your colleagues get a chance to use the best of what is in your personal inventories. Focusing on strengths (not weaknesses) and looking for what you have in common (rather than what you disagree on) is usually the best way to move the group to consensus. The best way to create this environment is for you to be a role model for the rest of the group. If you focus on your best attributes and those of others and you work to leave your undesirable baggage behind, you will have packed smartly for your trip to Consensusville.

> **Idea:** "We must be the change we wish to see in the world."
> —Gandhi

Think of the last time that you were involved in a group.

*What did you add to the group that is uniquely you?* _____

_____

*What are your best skills?* _____

_____

*How did you use them to their fullest?* _____

_____

*Did you encourage working to consensus? If you didn't, why not?* _____

_____

*Will you be willing to do so now?* _____

_____

You have taken a hard look at the items that you want to bring on your journey to Consensusville. You have a better understanding of what will aid you in your journey and what will hold you back.

# III

# Meeting to Achieve Consensus

## Planning Checklist

☐ Choose Your Destination

☐ Decide What to Pack

☑ **Understand Your Traveling Companions**

☑ **Select Your Route**

☐ Prepare to Tackle Any Roadblock or Obstacle

# YOU CAN'T ACHIEVE CONSENSUS BY YOURSELF

*"We must indeed all hang together, or, most assuredly, we shall all hang separately."*

—Benjamin Franklin

Earlier you learned about yourself and how individuals' skills and experience affect the consensus process. Now it is time to take that knowledge and put it into action. The forum for putting your skills into action will most likely be a meeting.

---

### *Planning Checklist*

☐ Choose Your Destination

☐ Decide What to Pack

☑ **Understand Your Traveling Companions**

☑ **Select Your Route**

☐ Prepare to Tackle Any Roadblock or Obstacle

---

Let's begin by reviewing the top-level consensus process (see diagram on next page). First, people with different ideas and different approaches get together. They work to agree on what problem they want to resolve. Then, they work together to define a solution that everyone in the group can support. The output of the group is a solution that will be effective because the group owns it.

# YOU CAN'T ACHIEVE CONSENSUS BY YOURSELF (continued)

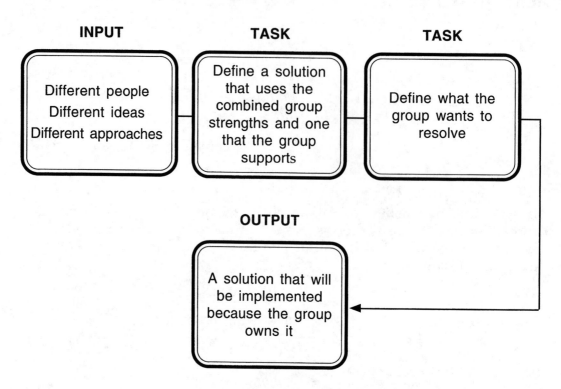

**INPUT**

Different people
Different ideas
Different approaches

**TASK**

Define a solution that uses the combined group strengths and one that the group supports

**TASK**

Define what the group wants to resolve

**OUTPUT**

A solution that will be implemented because the group owns it

Although this process may appear simple, the way that people come together in groups is not. If you take the time to understand how this process works, you can make a positive impact in your next group.

*How would you describe how groups you have participated in come together?*

_____

_____

*Assess its effectiveness?* _____

_____

*Was there a feeling of randomness or disorganization to the process?* _____

_____

# LET'S MAKE STEEL

Think of the way that people come together to work to consensus as being similar to the process of making steel. Steel is a strong metal, but to make it, you have to start with something else. To make steel, you start with iron.

Iron is the fourth most common element in the earth's crust. By itself, iron is brittle and rusts easily. Iron is useful, but steel is stronger and more valuable. Yet iron, when handled in a certain way, turns into steel.

When you make steel, you have to **mix** the iron with the proper metals, **melt** everything together and then **mold** the liquid steel into whatever you are making. The end result is something that surpasses its beginnings. People, working to consensus, can achieve similar results if they **mix, melt** and **mold**.

## Phase I: The Mix

Mixing comes first. Even if you are not the leader of the group, you can play a valuable role. During this part of the process you should focus on:

> **Getting the Group Started**
>
> **Ensuring Appropriate Representation**
>
> **Setting Up "Rules of the Road"**
>
> **Agreeing on "Why We Are Here"**
>
> **Agreeing on "Commitment"**

Let's discuss each of these items.

# LET'S MAKE STEEL (continued)

## Getting the Group Started

Perhaps you have been selected as the leader and need to get your new group together, or perhaps you have been asked to help. You need to get the participants selected and invited, arrange for a meeting place, and prepare people for the first meeting by providing any required information. Be sensitive to meeting locations. The time and location of your meeting can help or hurt the chance of a successful meeting. Even the furniture layout can affect your meeting. Pick a neutral location where you will not be interrupted. Arrange for seating either in a circle or a U shape. It is usually better to meet in the morning than afternoon. Before the meeting, arrange for someone to take notes for you so you will be free to concentrate on the meeting.

**HINT:** You only get one chance to make a first impression. Make sure that the impression you create is one of caring and attention to detail.

*Have you considered the impact of the meeting site's physical layout?*

☐ Yes ☐ No     If "No," did you notice any impact?

*Have you participated in meetings that were not in a neutral area?*

☐ Yes ☐ No     If "Yes," did you notice any impact?

## Ensuring Appropriate Representation

When you select people to attend the meeting, make sure that all pertinent areas are represented. Ask the group if they feel that all areas are represented. If no, then take steps to correct the situation. From the beginning, even if you are not the leader, you set the tone by asking: "Do we need anyone else before we move on?"

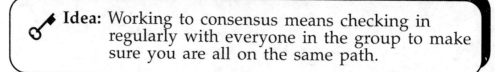

**Idea:** Working to consensus means checking in regularly with everyone in the group to make sure you are all on the same path.

*Have you ensured that every essential area was represented?*

☐ Yes ☐ No    If "No," did you notice any impact?

## Setting Up Rules of the Road

New groups become more productive quicker if participants agree to standards of conduct. This code of conduct sets the expectation for the members of the group concerning what is acceptable and what is not in their dealings with each other. All members of the group should participate in creating the Rules of the Road and all members should agree to them. Even if you are not the leader of the group, you can be an advocate for the group needing and creating these standards of conduct. Once the rules are decided, you can ask, "Does each member feel comfortable with these rules?" or "Is everyone prepared to follow these rules?" Check in with yourself and with your group members.

Some typical Rules of the Road might be:

## *Rules of the Road*

- Everyone gets a chance to participate
- All ideas have value
- Everyone arrives on time
- All members come prepared
- No personal attacks
- Build on people's ideas, do not tear them down
- If we make a mistake, we will fix it
- Discussion of ideas is encouraged
- Decisions are made by consensus
- No alternates for absent members are allowed
- We work with facts and data
- If we can't measure it, we can't manage it

# LET'S MAKE STEEL (continued)

*Can you think of any other rules to add to the list?*

☐ Yes  ☐ No    If "Yes," what are they?

_____

_____

> 🔑 **Idea:** It helps to put your Rules of the Road on a poster and keep it visible during your meetings.

## Agreeing on "Why We Are Here"

The group came together for a reason, but what is that reason? Usually there are as many ideas on why we are here as there are people in the group. Until participants share a common understanding and agreement on the purpose of the group, they will be little progress. This common agreement on the purpose of the group can be called the "charter" or "mission" or "objective" or "goal" of the group. Although each of these words may mean something slightly different, don't get obsessed with terminology. The important point is to make sure that everyone understands and agrees why the group exists. You can help by suggesting that groups have a better chance of being successful if they:

✓ Document the group's purpose in writing with all the members of the group participating.

✓ Check with each member of the group to make sure they understand the group's purpose.

✓ Check with each member of the group to make sure they agree with the group's purpose.

✓ Do not go on until these steps are done.

# EXERCISE: *True/False*

Read the following questions and check either True or False. Check your
answers against those in the box at the bottom of the page.

|  | True | False |
|---|---|---|
| 1. Deciding on the problem to be solved is the easiest part of the decision-making process. | ☐ | ☐ |
| 2. Even if you are not the group's leader, you can play a valuable role. | ☐ | ☐ |
| 3. The time and location of a meeting can help or hurt your success. | ☐ | ☐ |
| 4. It is usually most productive to hold meetings in the leader's office. | ☐ | ☐ |
| 5. Late afternoon is the most effective time to hold meetings. | ☐ | ☐ |
| 6. Make sure that all pertinent areas are represented. | ☐ | ☐ |
| 7. The first thing the leader should do to ensure a quick start is to present members with the Rules of the Road. | ☐ | ☐ |
| 8. By the time a group forms, all members have a clear idea of why they are there. | ☐ | ☐ |

**Answers:** 1. F, 2. T, 3. T, 4. F, 5. F, 6. T, 7. T, 8. F

# LET'S MAKE STEEL (continued)

## Agreeing On Commitment

A group of people can agree on a common purpose, but if they do not commit to the effort, the group can still fail to achieve its goal. Questions to ask include:

- How many hours a week will you work on this project?
- What other resources are you willing to use for this task?
- What resources do we need for this group to succeed?
- How much time do we have?
- How much time do we need?

You can help by working to get the answers. At each step, make sure that the group agrees with the outcome and document it.

> **Idea:** Writing things down is one of the most effective tools to make sure you don't waste time on items already covered.

## Performing Joint Fact Finding

Nothing ruins a good argument or an unreasonable position like facts and data. Nothing brings diverse people together like a quest for the truth. Intermingle the group members so that diverse views are represented for each portion of the group doing the fact finding. Make sure that fact finders represent a mix of skills and experience. Mix people together. Two things will happen.

1. They will get to know each other, which will increase the chance that they will be open to new ideas.

2. They will see how they arrived at the facts and data and will be more likely to believe it and advocate it to the rest of the group.

Some people refer to the fact-finding step as documenting the "as-is," which means that we examine the situation just as it is. We are not worried about solutions, only about getting information that can help us arrive at a good solution. Once fact finding is underway, the group starts the "melt" phase of the consensus process.

## Phase II: The Melt

Just as iron has to be heated to transform it into steel, people must go through a period where their ideas and ways of looking at the world are challenged. *This challenging of ideas, perceptions and assumptions is a critical point in the consensus building process.* If the group doesn't generate any heat, it won't find any light, and the group will stay stuck in the status quo. But if conflicts are not handled properly, then tempers can flare, people can feel intimated and the consensus process can come to a halt.

Here is what you can do to help during the Melt part of the process.

> **Realize That You're Only Human**
>
> **Put Yourself in the Other Person's Shoes**
>
> **Question, Listen and Repeat**
>
> **Address All Issues**

# LET'S MAKE STEEL (continued)

## Realize That You're Only Human

Before you can help others work to consensus, you need to know yourself. You have vested interests and emotions. You bring these things with you. The best thing that you can do for yourself is to realize that you are only human and then become aware of what your "triggers" are. Triggers are things that produce an emotional response from you. If you know your triggers, you can choose your response instead of always acting the same way. Once you have yourself figured out, you can work to set an example for the rest of the group. Even then, remember that group members are only human. Let everyone have his or her say before you start discussing options or solutions. People listen and work together better after they have been heard. Let people get their issues out in the open. Don't defend while participants communicate their issues and emotions. Realize that just because someone says it does not make it true, but also realize that if the other person believes it to be true, it is true for him or her. Discuss why someone believes what he or she says. Use this time as a chance to learn about the interests, hopes and fears of the other members of the group.

## Put Yourself in the Other Person's Shoes

People tend to look only for things that support their position and ignore the rest. If you want to help create options and solutions that benefit the whole group, you need to understand what the other people believe. Do not project your values, experiences and beliefs on others. Ask questions to understand what they feel. The groups most likely to work to consensus are those that value diversity in experiences and beliefs and take the time and energy necessary to understand those differences.

> **Idea:** Think of yourself as a detective trying to understand why the members of the group act the way they do. Let them talk so that you may better understand.

## Question, Listen and Repeat

The best way to a common understanding is to ask questions, listen to the person's answer and repeat what you think you heard. Even if you think you know the answer, other people in the group may need to hear it. If you do only one thing to help bring the group to consensus, remember "Question, Listen and Repeat."

> **Idea:** Ask a *Question, Listen* to the answer and *Repeat* what you understood. This action sets the tone for everyone else.

## Address All Issues

During the Melt phase of the consensus process, people may choose to ignore the major or difficult issues. Make sure that you and all the other members of the group get your issues, concerns, fears or hopes addressed. If issues are not handled here, then the group will be making decisions based on incomplete or faulty information. This is one of the biggest challenges that you face in your group. You have to check with yourself and with your group members periodically.

*"Are your issues being addressed?"*

or

*"Is there anything else that we need to discuss before we move on?"*

or

*"You still seem uneasy about . . ."*

If the issues do not come out here, they will come out later, usually during final decision making or implementation. If the issues come out too late, then considerable time and effort is wasted. Do it now, during the Melt. Once people have discussed their issues, they are ready to start the Mold portion of the process.

42

# LET'S MAKE STEEL (continued)

## EXERCISE: *True/False*

Read the following questions and check either True or False. Check your answers against those in the box at the bottom of the page.

|  | True | False |
|---|---|---|
| 1. Make sure that fact finders represent a mix of skills. | ☐ | ☐ |
| 2. It is important to keep the focus on the solution at all times. | ☐ | ☐ |
| 3. The process of challenging ideas is usually what causes most consensus-building failures. | ☐ | ☐ |
| 4. It is most productive for people to explore their triggers in a group with others around. | ☐ | ☐ |
| 5. Emotions are neither right nor wrong. | ☐ | ☐ |
| 6. Limit each person's talking time to ensure quick problem resolution. | ☐ | ☐ |
| 7. It is common for people to ignore difficult issues. | ☐ | ☐ |
| 8. One of your major challenges is to make sure that everyone's issues are addressed. | ☐ | ☐ |

Answers: 1. T, 2. F, 3. F, 4. F, 5. T, 6. F, 7. T, 8. T

# Phase III: The Mold

The Mold portion of consensus building is where things start to come together. Just as the molten steel was poured into the die to shape it, the team, working to consensus, has now started to make progress toward the desired solution. Ideas are forming and taking shape. Options are shaped and reshaped with the team's facts and data. During the Mold portion of the process you should:

> **Focus On the Group's Desired Outcomes, Not Individual Solutions**
>
> **Predefine the Options-Rating Criteria**
>
> **Create Many Options**
>
> **All for One and One for All**

# LET'S MAKE STEEL (continued)

## Focus On the Group's Desired Outcomes, Not Individual Solutions

### *Focusing On the Outcome: A Parable*

Two young sisters worked in the kitchen. Each said that she needed a lemon for her recipe. One sister was making pudding and the other a cake. Each recipe called for one lemon; but there was only one lemon to be had. They tried to decide who would get the one lemon. Each talked about how her need for the lemon was more important. Each threatened the other about what would happen if she did not get her way. Hours were wasted and they were not one step closer to deciding who should get the lemon. Finally, their mother arrived and asked each to explain the problem. One sister explained how she needed the juice of the lemon to make her lemon pudding. The other sister described how she needed the rind of the lemon to add to the lemon cake she was making. The mother listened carefully. She took the lemon, and grated the rind to get the zest and lemon essence of the peel for her daughter making the cake. Next, she cut the lemon in two and squeezed out the juice and gave it to her daughter making the pudding. One lemon was enough for everyone, once the desired outcomes were fully understood.

Several lessons can be learned from this story.

► If you focus on the desired outcomes instead of demanding your own solution, you stand a better chance of finding a compromise that everyone can support.

► Make sure that your desired outcomes are as specific as possible, because the more specific they are, the better chance your group can make it real.

► Each member of the group usually has several desired outcomes. Let everyone get his or her major desired outcomes out on the table.

## Predefine the Options-Rating Criteria

Once you have identified the desired outcomes, the next step is to find an objective way of rating the options against a list of criteria. Remember, you have not begun to define options yet.

When software programmers design a new program, the first thing they do is define the requirements (desired outcomes) for the software program. Then they define the testing (options-rating criteria) that will be done to determine if the software program meets the requirements. This approach helps with the option creation process because it identifies important criteria. As you get the criteria listed, check with yourself and each member of the group to ensure that each supports all items.

> **Idea:** Criteria development gives you something to measure your solution against and makes you think about what is important before you start with solutions.

## EXERCISE: True/False

Read the following questions and check either True or False. Check your answers against those in the box at the bottom of the page.

|  | True | False |
|---|---|---|
| 1. Focus on individual solutions; they are your key to success. | ☐ | ☐ |
| 2. Make sure desired outcomes are as general as possible. | ☐ | ☐ |
| 3. Find a way to rate your options against a list of criteria. | ☐ | ☐ |
| 4. Each member usually has one preferred outcome. | ☐ | ☐ |
| 5. Criteria development gives you something to measure your solution against. | ☐ | ☐ |

**Answers:** 1. F, 2. F, 3. T, 4. F, 5. T

# LET'S MAKE STEEL (continued)

## Create Many Options

The two biggest problems that occur during this part of the process are that people limit themselves and offer premature judgments. Nothing kills the group's progress faster than the person who constantly offers "That will never work" or "No way will this ever get accepted." Put off limited thinking and judging while you create options. You will have plenty of time for that when you compare your options to the criteria. This is the time to have fun. Brainstorm ideas and options. Suggest options that are totally against your requirements to demonstrate your willingness to get all options out on the table. Play with the options by combining aspects of each. Pretend that you are in a different profession and ask yourself what options you would present. If you are working on an engineering problem, ask yourself how a farmer would solve the problem. Sometimes silly things lead to a different way of solving a problem.

## All for One and One for All

The Three Musketeers are legendary. These three adventurers, working together, could take on twice as many adversaries and still win the battle. How could they do this? Their rallying cry was "All for One and One for All." They worked together. They shared a common goal and they made a commitment to that goal.

Your group may never be as famous as the Three Musketeers, but your group can achieve seemingly impossible tasks. Focus on taking all the information you have gathered so far and put it into a solution that all in the group can support. If you have followed the process of Mix, Melt, and Mold, then you should be at a point where it is relatively easy to form a solution that all the group can support. You will have reached Consensusville. Congratulations!

## What to Expect at this Phase

It would be nice if every group that got together to work to consensus followed the mix, melt and mold consensus-building process; but each group is different. Some groups may never get to melt. Some groups get into Melt and get stuck. One thing is constant—you can expect problems. Now you can also start to do something about them.

# ARE YOU A CONSENSUS MASTER?

Whether you are the group leader or a group member, you can create and support a consensus-oriented environment.

▶ *Ask what decision style the group will use to reach decisions.*

Advocate consensus. Be prepared to educate the rest of the group as to why you advocate consensus. As a group, agree on the decision style. Now everyone will know how things will be decided and will feel more ownership.

▶ *Ask the group to define why everyone is there.*

Put it in writing. Make sure that all in the group agree to the reason or "mission" of the group. This will focus your work and the group will be more effective.

▶ *Gather information before making a decision.*

This will allow you and others a chance to participate and share information. The more the group can focus on commonly generated information and work together toward a group decision, the less likely that any one person will force through a win-lose position.

▶ *Ask for other people's ideas.*

Encourage novel approaches and perspectives. Encourage those in positions of power to hold their ideas until last so that everyone gets a chance to participate. Make sure that *all* positions are heard and explored. Just because all ideas are communicated does not mean you have to agree with them.

▶ *Be honest with yourself and the group.*

Be aware of your own thoughts and biases on the issues. If you have concerns, speak up. Don't wait until the meeting is over and then complain in the hallway.

▶ *Always check in with yourself and the group.*

Ask if the decision is something that you and everyone in the group can support.

# EXERCISE: *True/False*

Read the following questions and check either True or False. Check your answers against those in the box at the bottom of the page.

|  | True | False |
|---|:---:|:---:|
| 1. Put off limited thinking and judging while you are creating options. | ☐ | ☐ |
| 2. Have fun and brainstorm ideas and solutions. | ☐ | ☐ |
| 3. Having the group decide on a decision style is a fast way to ensure disaster. | ☐ | ☐ |
| 4. People support that which they help create. | ☐ | ☐ |
| 5. Suppress novel approaches, as it gets people off target and slows down the process. | ☐ | ☐ |
| 6. After meeting, and in private, is best for voicing concerns. | ☐ | ☐ |

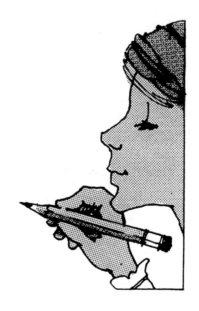

Answers: 1. T, 2. T, 3. F, 4. T, 5. F, 6. F

# SELF-REVIEW

Let's look at how you are performing as a consensus role model. Review each statement in the left-hand column of the chart below, then circle the word in the right-hand column that best describes how you think you are doing.

| | A | B | C | D | E |
|---|---|---|---|---|---|
| 1. I arrive prepared to discuss the issue | Always | Often | Sometimes | Seldom | Never |
| 2. Before coming to the meeting, I do my homework and am prepared to explain my position | Always | Often | Sometimes | Seldom | Never |
| 3. During the discussion, I say what is on my mind | Always | Often | Sometimes | Seldom | Never |
| 4. I stay focused on the purpose of the decision | Always | Often | Sometimes | Seldom | Never |
| 5. Opinions that are different from mine are a positive part of the discussion | Always | Often | Sometimes | Seldom | Never |
| 6. Throughout the discussion, I help clarify what has been said and make sure all points have been heard | Always | Often | Sometimes | Seldom | Never |
| 7. I avoid the urge to rush to an immediate solution | Always | Often | Sometimes | Seldom | Never |
| 8. I address conflict when it surfaces in the discussion | Always | Often | Sometimes | Seldom | Never |
| 9. I work for the best decision, not just my preferred choice | Always | Often | Sometimes | Seldom | Never |
| 10. When conflicts arise, I confront ideas and issues, not people | Always | Often | Sometimes | Seldom | Never |
| 11. I express my views honestly without attacking anyone else | Always | Often | Sometimes | Seldom | Never |
| 12. I agree with the final decision only if I plan to support its implementation | Always | Often | Sometimes | Seldom | Never |

*Scoring Instructions.* Count the number of responses circled from each column on the right-hand side of the page (the number of As, Bs, etc.). Put those numbers in the "# of Responses" blanks below. Then, multiply that figure by the number in the multiplier column to calculate your subtotals. Add the subtotals to reach your final score.

## *Your Consensus Tally Sheet*

| Subcolumn | # of Responses | Multiplier | Subtotal |
|-----------|----------------|------------|----------|
| A | _____ | × 5 | _____ |
| B | _____ | × 4 | _____ |
| C | _____ | × 3 | _____ |
| D | _____ | × 2 | _____ |
| E | _____ | × 1 | _____ |
| | | **TOTAL:** | _____ |

| Score | Rating |
|-------|--------|
| 52–60 | **Consensus Master.** People want you to participate in groups because of your excellent consensus skills. |
| 44–51 | **Consensus Builder.** You use your skills consistently and are an asset to your groups. |
| 34–43 | **Consensus Seeker.** You are having some success with consensus, but are seeking ways to grow your skills. |
| 21–33 | **Consensus Novice.** The path ahead of you is full of opportunity. |
| 11–20 | **Consensus Dreamer.** Consensus will be more than a dream after you try some of the ideas in this book. |
| 0–10 | **Impossible.** Add again! |

Although you have learned the theory of how to structure your meetings to achieve consensus, now you need to learn what to do when things don't go as planned.

# P A R T

# IV

# Tools and Techniques

# USING YOUR TOOL KIT

*"We are not primarily put on this earth to see through one another, but to see one another through."*

—Peter DeVries

We know that everything does not always go as planned. At that point, it is helpful to have tools that will help to overcome the obstacles you confront on your way. You can be the guide using the tools and techniques that follow.

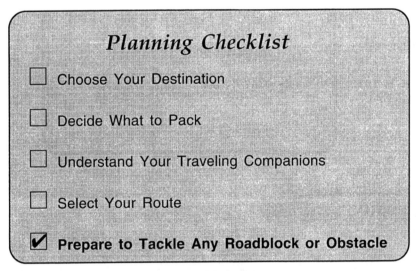

*Planning Checklist*

☐ Choose Your Destination

☐ Decide What to Pack

☐ Understand Your Traveling Companions

☐ Select Your Route

☑ **Prepare to Tackle Any Roadblock or Obstacle**

# ADDRESSING BEHAVIORAL OBSTACLES

> Personality Conflicts
>
> Dominating Behavior
>
> Anger
>
> Withholding Information
>
> Lack of Participation
>
> Unresolvable Conflict
>
> Missing Commitments
>
> Unwilling to Compromise

## Personality Conflicts

Many people believe that conflict is negative and destructive to the consensus process, but nothing could be further from the truth. Conflict can be a powerful source of creativity and innovation. The secret to using conflict positively is to manage it. To use conflict as a positive source of change, acknowledge that conflict exists. Avoiding the situation may escalate bad feelings, so acknowledgment is a critical step.

Next, accept responsibility. Every person is responsible for his or her behavior, and no one engages in conflict alone. If the conflict is between you and another person, address it with him or her outside of the meeting time. Talk about your behavior and concerns. State clearly that you wish to resolve the issue and move forward. Ask for the other person's help in resolving the disagreement. Be willing to take the first step toward resolution.

If the conflict is between other members of your group, bring it up as an issue. Ask if the people involved wish to resolve the concern. Help them to find even a small point of agreement and use that as a building block for resolution. Failing to manage conflict can be a death sentence to the consensus process. If your group decides they cannot manage conflict alone, get outside help. A neutral facilitator can offer a perspective that may have been overlooked by those involved.

> **Idea:** Watch for "violent agreement." Violent agreement is where two people say the same thing but are so passionate about their point of view that they don't listen to each other.

*How can you demonstrate your focus on the partnership of consensus?* _____

## Dominating Behavior

Dominating behaviors include:

- Aggression

- Disagreeing without apparent reason

- Controlling the group's discussion

- Speaking for other members of the group without their consent

People who display dominating behavior may be unaware of the effect of their behavior on the group and may feel they are simply "moving things along" at a quicker pace. They may just want to get on with it and believe that the group is wasting time.

# ADDRESSING BEHAVIORAL OBSTACLES (continued)

It is important to provide feedback to people who engage in dominating behaviors. Pay special attention to avoid blaming the person and address the specific behavior only. Be sure and let the person know how their behavior is affecting you or the group.

*Example:* *"Brook, when you interrupt the discussion and don't let people finish, people back away, and we might not get all the issues addressed."*

You may also want to understand why this person uses dominating behavior. If you understand the reason, perhaps you can do something to address the root cause and the behavior will go away. Possible reasons include:

- Not feeling heard by the group

- Finding opposing suggestions threatening

- Seeing group as deferring to someone else's wishes

The Rules of the Road help to manage dominating behavior. Everyone in the group deserves an equal chance to be heard and to express themselves. Remind the dominator of the Rules.

Many times the leader of the group is the one who dominates. This person may feel responsible for the group's success and may want to push to keep the group going. Define the role of the leader to ensure the entire group's participation. One effective technique to use with the leader is to ask that they speak after everyone else has spoken. Another technique is to record how much time each person speaks. Pick any meeting and keep a rough tally of time. You can then offer this information to the group to suggest possible changes.

# EXERCISE: True/False

Read the following questions and check either True or False. Check your answers against those in the box at the bottom of the page.

|  | True | False |
|---|---|---|
| **1.** Conflict is negative. | ☐ | ☐ |
| **2.** People who dominate often feel threatened. | ☐ | ☐ |
| **3.** Insist that the other person initiate conflict resolution. | ☐ | ☐ |
| **4.** A neutral facilitator is sometimes a good option for resolving conflict. | ☐ | ☐ |
| **5.** Controlling the group's discussion is a critical function of the team leader. | ☐ | ☐ |
| **6.** Leaders should speak after everyone else has been heard. | ☐ | ☐ |

If you don't know the
answers, reread this section!

**Answers:** 1. F, 2. T, 3. F, 4. T, 5. F, 6. T

# ADDRESSING BEHAVIORAL OBSTACLES (continued)

### Handling Anger

Managing our own anger can be challenging, and it can be doubly difficult to handle someone else's. A situation that raises anger in one person may have no effect on another. Thus, it's clear that anger is self-generated. If it is self-generated then it should be something that is under our control. If only it were that easy! It is helpful to think of anger as energy. You can channel that energy into destructive behaviors or allow it to help you create a positive outcome.

## *Three Keys to Understanding Anger*

1. Be responsible for how you choose to feel. People often give away their power by blaming someone else for their feelings. Others may do things that make it easy to *choose* to feel angry, but it is still your choice.

2. Focus on the issue rather than the emotion when responding to another's anger. Maintain your calm and do not respond to anger with anger.

3. Remember that anger is simply a release of emotional energy that expresses how deeply the conflict, issue or situation affects you. This is valuable information that can be used to help resolve issues. Just because someone is angry does not mean they aren't interested in resolving the issue. The consensus process requires that we express our feelings so that resolution can be reached.

*What are your hot buttons or areas that need improvement?* _____

_____

*Are you willing to ask other people for help?* _____

_____

## Withholding Information

People withhold information from their group discussions when they perceive a positive outcome for doing so. Is recognition given for personal achievement that puts this group member in competition with the others? Was information previously shared and the group responded negatively?

When people express their opinions, they become accountable for them. Expressing yourself helps to eliminate confusion and clarify expectations. If anyone seems to hold back information, question the behavior to try to understand its cause.

*Example:* *"Lee, you have a lot of experience in this area, but lately you have had little to say. Has the group done anything to make you uncomfortable expressing your opinions?"*

You may find it helpful to focus on the rewards that will be gained by your group's reaching consensus. Each member's full sharing of information is essential to a successful outcome.

## Lack of Participation

Quiet members often need to develop trust with the group before they feel comfortable sharing ideas and opinions. A small dose of criticism may appear large to a person who fears failure or ridicule. Encourage these members and respond positively to their efforts. Asking open-ended questions helps to initiate conversation.

*Example:* *"We have heard from nearly everyone on this issue. Jo, you have a lot of experience with this, what do you think?"*

All types of people will be in your groups and people need the space to be who they are. Not every person is talkative. But because consensus requires everyone's buy-in, hearing from the quiet people is imperative. Don't assume that silence is agreement—ask!

# ADDRESSING BEHAVIORAL OBSTACLES (continued)

> 🗝 **Idea:** When coming to a decision, ask each person for comments. Do not ask for a show of hands. Go around the room, person by person, and wait for individual comments.

## EXERCISE: *True/False*

Read the following questions and check either True or False. Check your answers against those in the box at the bottom of the page.

|  | True | False |
|---|:---:|:---:|
| 1. People often give away their power by blaming someone else for their feelings. | ☐ | ☐ |
| 2. Anger is self-generated. | ☐ | ☐ |
| 3. People who are angry are not interested in reaching consensus. | ☐ | ☐ |
| 4. Holding back information is common. | ☐ | ☐ |
| 5. Focus on the rewards gained by reaching consensus. | ☐ | ☐ |
| 6. Close-ended questions are best for initiating conversations. | ☐ | ☐ |
| 7. It is imperative to replace nontalkative people with others who are better able to communicate. | ☐ | ☐ |

**Answers:** 1. T, 2. T, 3. F, 4. T, 5. T, 6. F, 7. F

## Unresolvable Conflict

Don't accept the idea that conflict is unresolvable, so you can give up or move on. If problems are not addressed, you will pay for them sooner or later. Conflicts are not resolved because:

► One or more of the people is unskilled in conflict resolution

► One or more of the people does not wish to resolve the conflict

The goal of consensus is to reach a decision that meets individual and group needs and addresses the reason the group got together in the first place. It is too easy to decide that the goal is unattainable and settle for a short-term solution in which one party defeats the others. The problem with this is that the chance for a successful implementation is reduced. Even if the solution is implemented, it will not address all the needs of the group.

Some conflicts truly are more difficult to resolve than others—especially when values, power issues or incompatible needs are involved. Agreement that the group wants to resolve the conflict is the first step. Finding common ground that the group can build on is the next step. Expand on areas of agreement rather than focusing on disagreement.

 **Idea:** Check to see if members still agree on the goal. If not, ask each person to explain what they disagree with and why. Then ask them what could be done to remove the disagreement.

When all of this has been done and the light at the end of the tunnel is still the headlight of an oncoming train, you may want to seek an outside facilitator. Don't allow this conflict to destroy the possibility of success in the future. Amazing results have been achieved through determination.

*What will you need to do to increase your comfort level with conflict?* _____

# ADDRESSING BEHAVIORAL OBSTACLES (continued)

## Missing Commitments

When you or other members of the group miss commitments made to the group, it may be simply a problem of priorities or it may have a more complex source. This problem is often overlooked in the consensus process. It is a warning sign for future problems.

Making your commitments is key for your group to reach consensus. If you don't do what you what you say you will do, how can you expect people to trust you? How will your group get anything done? You can judge how your group is doing by focusing on *interim commitments*. If people don't meet the small commitments, it is likely the investment is missing for the overall goal. Address this issue as soon as you become aware of it. Asking questions can shed a lot of light on the problem.

► Is the person feeling left out, ignored, unappreciated?

► Are the frustrations with how the group is operating?

► Is the person no longer interested in the issue?

► Is the member overextended?

The key to overcoming this obstacle is addressing the issue and agreeing on what level of commitment is acceptable to everyone involved. When agreement is reached, stick to it. Once missing commitments becomes a standard operating procedure for your group, it is hard to recover and get the commitment necessary to reach consensus.

 **Idea:** You can be a positive role model. Do what you say and say what you'll do.

## Unwilling to Compromise

This obstacle is easy to recognize because the behavior screams, "I want my own way!" People like to have their own way some of the time, but this becomes a problem when someone needs their own way all of the time. When overcoming this obstacle, remember that just because someone wants *their* way, doesn't mean you have to dig in your heels to get *your* way. Explore why a person might act in this fashion. This behavior usually surfaces when:

► *The person doesn't understand that consensus is not an I-versus-you struggle.*

Focus on shared needs and shared power when addressing this behavior. Consensus requires partners rather than adversaries, so maintain a positive atmosphere when discussing issues. Challenge the people involved to find a path to resolution that improves the relationship for all involved.

► *The person believes that if others are heard, their ideas may be considered; thus, power will be lost.*

When you use consensus, keep the focus on developing "our" power. The power of the group is much stronger that the power of any single member and this point should be reinforced.

► *The person may be focusing on his or her own control over the situation instead of the needs of the situation.*

Encourage the member to address options relating to proposed solutions rather than controlling a single or specific outcome. It is not possible to reach consensus by giving in to one member's desire to avoid conflict. The immediate situation may go away, but the relationship will not improve and neither of you has learned to resolve conflict. Think of consensus as a partnership—finding a resolution that is "getting *our* way!"

# ADDRESSING BEHAVIORAL OBSTACLES
## (continued)

### EXERCISE: *True/False*

Read the following questions and check either True or False. Check your answers against those in the box at the bottom of the page.

|  | True | False |
|---|:---:|:---:|
| 1. If problems are not addressed, you will have a better chance at consensus. | ☐ | ☐ |
| 2. Focus on areas of disagreement. | ☐ | ☐ |
| 3. Some people might not want to resolve conflict. | ☐ | ☐ |
| 4. If you get stuck, ask members for their solutions. | ☐ | ☐ |
| 5. Missing commitments is a warning sign that the group might be in trouble. | ☐ | ☐ |
| 6. People like to have their own way. | ☐ | ☐ |
| 7. Some people view consensus as an I-versus-you struggle. | ☐ | ☐ |
| 8. Be quick to help others overcome negative positions. | ☐ | ☐ |

**Answers:** 1. F, 2. F, 3. T, 4. T, 5. T, 6. T, 7. T, 8. F (work on yourself)

# YOUR ROLE

The first place to address the problems listed in this chapter is with you. Make sure you provide a positive model to the rest of the group. Check your suitcase to make sure that none of those items you wanted to leave behind came with you. Nothing is more exasperating than to have the worst offender preach to the rest of the group about how everyone else should clean up his or her act. Do the best that you can to be sensitive to your own actions. Ask others for direct, honest feedback. Pay attention to what they say and what they don't say. Do not be quick to help everyone else without considering areas you might need help in. If you need some help, ask for it.

*Example:* *"I know that I have a tendency to dominate the conversation and I'll try not do it. The next time that I run on, would someone please give me a sign?"*

*Are you willing to be the catalyst for positive change in your groups?* _____

*List several benefits to doing this.* _____

_____

*What is the one thing that you will do differently in your next meeting?* _____

_____

Stumbling blocks are a part of walking the path, so you needn't be surprised if you encounter a few. These obstacles can turn into brick walls if the knowledge or desire isn't present to work through them. With determination, your stumbling blocks can be surmounted.

# P A R T

# V

# More Tools
# and Techniques

## Planning Checklist

☐ **Choose Your Destination**

☐ **Decide What to Pack**

☐ **Understand Your Traveling Companions**

☐ **Select Your Route**

☑ **Prepare to Tackle Any Roadblock or Obstacle**

# USING YOUR TOOL KIT FOR DECISION OBSTACLES

*"We must not only give what we have;*
*we must also give what we are."*

—Cardinal Mercier

Unhelpful behavior is not the only obstacle that may confront you during your consensus process. Making decisions can present obstacles also. None of the obstacles is insurmountable, and by recognizing them as they occur you can help guide your group to successful resolution.

## Planning Checklist

☐ **Choose Your Destination**

☐ **Decide What to Pack**

☐ **Understand Your Traveling Companions**

☐ **Select Your Route**

☑ **Prepare to Tackle Any Roadblock or Obstacle**

# ADDRESSING DECISION OBSTACLES

> Missing Key Players
>
> Unbalanced Power Relationships
>
> Splinter Groups
>
> Getting Information
>
> Time Pressure
>
> Endless Discussion
>
> Losing Focus
>
> Indecisiveness
>
> Lack of Agreement

## Missing Key Players

The quality of the decision your group reaches is directly affected by the people who participate. Just getting everyone who gets along well to join the group doesn't necessarily lead to the best decision. Careful evaluation is necessary at the beginning of the group to evaluate if the right people are present.

*Example: "Do we have everyone we need participating who will affect our ability to implement this decision?"*

Getting key people to join the group may, at times, involve a bit of a sales job. Often these key people are busy on other projects and may be reluctant to take on something additional. If your task is not critical to gain the support of key people, then the first question to ask is, "Should we attempt this project at this time?" Experience shows that you are better off getting the right people up front, even if it means delaying the start. If you attempt to do something *right now* without the *right people*, the odds are that you will end *right back* where you started.

If you discover well into your consensus process that someone important is missing from the group, address the issue immediately. The longer you wait, the more difficult it will be for this person to catch up with the group. If you add a person to your group midway through your process, expect that you will need to go through the Mix stage again. The new member has not had the benefit of the past assumptions and decisions that got the group to this point and be sure those are still valid. The value of having all the key players participating far outweighs the step back in the decision process. The goal is implementation—not just reaching consensus.

## Unbalanced Power Relationships

Sharing responsibility throughout the consensus process is key to a quality decision. This idea of shared responsibility is new to many people. They need the world to be black or white. They are more comfortable where one person is the boss. (Usually the person who still feels this way *is* the boss.) They realize, though, that they need to embrace new concepts, but sometimes they slip back into old habits.

Sometimes members of the group long for the days when they could defer to the boss and not worry about responsibility. Sometimes members of the group are angry with the old authority figures and relish a chance to get back at them. On one hand, you have people who normally have responsibility trying to learn how to share it. On the other hand, you have people who are uncomfortable with responsibility trying to figure out what to do with it. Lastly, you may have people who have never had responsibility trying to take more than their share.

# ADDRESSING DECISION OBSTACLES
## (continued)

## EXERCISE: Keeping the Balance

Keep a close watch for symptoms that may indicate a power imbalance.

|  | Yes | No |
|---|---|---|
| Do certain members have access to more information? | ☐ | ☐ |
| Do they share it or use it only to their advantage? | ☐ | ☐ |
| Do some have more experience than others? | ☐ | ☐ |
| Do they share it or use it only to their advantage? | ☐ | ☐ |
| Do certain members have more "connections"? | ☐ | ☐ |
| Do they use those connections for the good of the group or themselves? | ☐ | ☐ |
| Do people outside the group repeatedly turn to the same individuals as representatives of the group? | ☐ | ☐ |
| Do those individuals then draw in the rest of the group? | ☐ | ☐ |
| Do members automatically look to one person for a decision? | ☐ | ☐ |
| Does one person constantly make all the decisions? | ☐ | ☐ |

If you discover some of the patterns listed above, you can work to lessen the affect on the group.

Talk about what you observe, then develop a plan with the rest of the group members that may include:

## *Plan to Balance Participation*

✓ Redistribute tasks or information flow to get different members into the heart of activity

✓ Identify new faces to represent the group to outside areas

✓ Make an effort to change the pattern of discussion so those less vocal speak first

✓ Set up a time for those more knowledgeable to share information to bring everyone to the same level

✓ Rotate roles to allow everyone to share in leadership

✓ Sit in a circle, which promotes more balance participation

Managing how your group communicates can have a large impact on unbalanced power relationships. The key here is to take the steps to create a level playing field even if the boss is in the group!

## Splinter Groups

You will recognize these groups when they show up and take issue with your group's decision because they were not included and felt they should have been. To avoid having splinter groups surface, first include all the key players. Second, as hard as you may try to identify key players, occasionally some important people are mistakenly left out and your group will need to address the splinter group's concerns. Here are some steps you can take to keep your decision and implementation on track.

 Educate the splinter group on your decision and the assumptions behind it. Allow any new concerns to be documented.

Remember, good decisions will stand up to challenge. Do not be afraid to allow for reasonable challenges. Once the splinter group understands what is behind your decision, it may end here. If not . . .

# ADDRESSING DECISION OBSTACLES (continued)

 Reassemble original participants and consider any new concerns that the splinter group surfaces. Include a representative of the splinter group in your discussion.

If the concerns are legitimate, they can affect your implementation. Usually, minor adjustments are all that's necessary to get back on track.

## Getting Information

One of the initial stumbling blocks your group may encounter is in gathering information necessary to make a good decision. Here are some tips you can follow to help you gather what you need.

TIP ONE: Create a list of your information needs and identify people who may be able to assist you in getting that information. Sometimes the information is available through another department or organization; sometimes you have to gather information yourself. Stay focused on the information you need. If your original task is to see how many deliveries are late, do not get sidetracked into implementing a new computer system for the purchasing department just to automate data gathering.

 **Idea:** Go after the facts in the most straightforward manner. Your eyes and ears are your best information-gathering tools.

TIP TWO: Use what is called a *best practices study*. That means you look at how other groups or companies handled this type of a decision and how they gathered information. *There is nothing wrong with modeling something that has worked in the past.*

TIP THREE: Use the most varied number of information sources possible. If you have a tough decision in front of you, equip yourself with facts. Don't rule out sources outside your company or organization. You can use universities, civic organizations, government agencies, vendors and customers.

TIP FOUR: Beware of paralysis by analysis. Know when enough is enough. At this point, there should be enough information available so that no one feels that their ideas have been ignored. Review what information you have. Ask, "What is the worst thing that will happen if I make a wrong decision based on the information I have now?" If the risk is something you can live with, then consider making a decision and making course corrections as you go along.

## Time Pressure

It would be nice to think that your group had all the time you desired to come to consensus, but that is almost never reality. Groups accept time pressures that are set internally (they do it to themselves) and externally (someone else imposes it on them). Most time constraints are false. If the choice is to make a poor decision quickly or a quality decision over a little more time, what would most people choose?

When coping with impossible time pressures—question, question, question. Why do we have only (one, three, five) meetings to come to consensus? Who is setting the constraint and what information would they need to reconsider? What is the worst that could happen if we cannot meet the time constraint?

If the time constraint is externally imposed, gather the necessary information and make a clear, specific request for more time. Point out the potential pitfalls in implementation if enough time is not spent in decision making.

On the other hand, having no time constraints or too generous a schedule can reduce the chance of ever reaching consensus. There is nothing like a deadline to help people focus on what is important to them.

# ADDRESSING DECISION OBSTACLES (continued)

Once you have questioned the time constraints, lay out a plan for your group to reach consensus in the shortest time possible. Remember, you can get from point A to point B on many routes—if you want the quickest way, get yourself a map and plot out the shortest course. The same is true for your group meetings. Develop a plan in the beginning to get from here to there. Have your members agree on it and then pick someone to help you stay on course. At the end of each meeting, check to see that your commitments are still in the proper priority. Eliminate tasks that you initially thought might add value, but now may not.

## Endless Discussion

Discussion, like conflict, is most valuable when managed. Keep track of where you are in a discussion—beginning, middle or end—and manage it appropriately.

In the beginning of the meeting, lay out a plan for how the discussion will proceed. Get agreement from the members first.

*Example:* *"We have agreed that Mary will record the key discussion points as we proceed. It's Bob's responsibility to watch for those points and highlight them to Mary and the group."*

In the middle of the discussion make sure everyone is participating and no single person is dominating. If the discussion seems to be circulating back on itself, take a poll that will allow your members to say where they stand on the issue based on the information they have right now. Often people are trying to convince each other when they are already in agreement.

*Example:* *"The discussion has been going over the same points for a while. Let's go around and take a poll to see what everyone would do if they had to decide now. We can continue the discussion if we don't all agree."*

In the final stages of the discussion summarize to bring closure. Suggest that one of the members pull together all the information that has already been discussed and provide a summary to the group.

*Example:* *"Betty, would you help us out and summarize the key thoughts. We can then allow 10 more minutes of discussion before asking for a decision. Is that acceptable to everyone?"*

Continue to push for closure until it is reached. Very often that push is just what a group needs to be successful.

## Losing Focus

It can happen quickly—your group is discussing one topic and without anyone noticing, the subject has changed. The new topic may be interesting, it may been be important to the final decision, but it needs its own time to be discussed.

To avoid getting off the subject and losing focus in your discussions, have a written agenda for each meeting. Set discussion time limits for each agenda item so the group can track progress.

*Example:* *"This appears to be an interesting topic, but we began with a discussion on performance feedback. Do we need to change the agenda or return to the original topic?"*

Watch for some of the typical problems that can take a group off track. Simultaneous discussions, a person providing more details than the topic warrants or dominating behavior can all work against the group's success. Identify the behavior you observe and offer an alternative to the group.

*Example:* *"George, you are very well informed on this topic. Perhaps you can help us by summarizing the key points at a high level so we can put them on the flip chart."*

When topics that are important, but off the current subject, are introduced, try parking them in the *parking lot*. To do this, first recognize the group is off topic. Then identify the subject that is off topic and suggest it be recorded on a separate listing for future discussions.

# ADDRESSING DECISION OBSTACLES (continued)

At the end of your meeting, revisit every topic that is in the parking lot and as a group decide if it belongs on a future agenda, is out of scope for your project or is something that needs to be worked on immediately. *Revisit the issues in the parking lot at the end of each meeting.* If you don't people will learn the parking lot is really the junk yard and it will have an extremely negative effect on the group.

## Indecisiveness

Indecisiveness usually occurs when either the goal is unclear or the path to reach the goal is unclear. You will first need to decide which is the case in order to provide the correct solution.

*Example:* *"We seem to be having difficulty reaching decisions. Let's revisit the goal to make sure that it is clear to everyone."*

If the goal is clarified but the difficulty persists, then . . .

*Example:* *"Let's decide on a process that will lead us to a decision. How about brainstorming our ideas and then prioritizing them?"*

If you have lots of ideas but are stuck with how to use them, try the multi-voting method of prioritization. List all of the ideas and then give each member three votes. Members can put all votes on one idea, two votes on one idea and a single vote on another, or spread the three votes on three ideas. Count all the votes and your priorities will surface. This process is not for the ultimate decision, but it will allow your group to see what people hold as most important and narrow the topics for discussion. After the top priorities are handled, the group can prioritize the remaining topics using the same technique.

You might find that your group can't make a decision because the members are afraid to make a mistake. If this is true for your group, discuss what would be necessary to create a *blame-free* and *risk-supportive* environment. Creating this kind of environment is critical to making quality decisions.

*Example:* *"Let's talk about what we are afraid will happen if we make a mistake. Then we can decide how to lessen the impact of what will happen."*

Remember, indecisiveness is usually a symptom of other problems. When you solve the problem, the symptom disappears.

## Lack of Agreement

Whenever you are caught in a web of disagreement, focus on the facts and not on the people. It's not about who is right—it's about what is right. When you reach a stalemate, go back to your data to help make a decision.

*Example:* *"We don't seem to be able to resolve the issue of developing new training manuals or using the existing ones. Let's go out to our customers and see what they would prefer."*

Consensus decision making does not require that every member must love the ultimate solution, only that they live with it and support its implementation. Often members are willing to reconsider a solution if the solution is presented with a reminder of the working definition of consensus.

*Example:* *"Let's find out where we stand on this solution. We'll go around the room and everyone can say whether they can live with it and are willing to support its implementation. If you are not, please let us know specifically what is the area of concern. We'll record those concerns and focus our future discussion on them."*

# ADDRESSING DECISION OBSTACLES
# (continued)

Managed disagreement and conflict are signs of a healthy group. If you get stuck, remember to use process solutions. Seek to find any possible common ground and use that as a starting point.

*Example:* *"It sounds like we all agree that the problem begins when we take the customer's order. Why don't we brainstorm all the potential issues in our Order Entry process and then we can prioritize them for discussion."*

Make sure that everyone has the same level of information as everyone else and all the assumptions are out on the table. Some topics are just plain tough to resolve, so give your group lots of encouragement as they work through their disagreements. If the group decides they can't resolve it alone, bring in someone from the outside to facilitate.

# WHEN ALL ELSE FAILS

When you have tried everything in your tool kit and you still feel that the group is stuck, ask the group:

▶ *Is this issue still worth solving?*

If yes, then the group has found common ground and reaffirmed their commitment to tackle the issue. If the answer is no, then perhaps the time is not right to continue. The only thing worse than not solving the issue is wasting everyone's time. Before giving up, ask if the group is willing to take some time to think about where we are and come back to the next meeting with at least one idea that we could use to get going again. Usually, the thought of "giving up after all this effort" is enough to get the group going again.

▶ *Can we test our way to consensus?*

Instead of arguing over how to proceed, can we agree to try any one of the options and let the results speak for themselves? If it doesn't work, then we can either modify it until it does work or try the next one until we find one that meets our desired outcome. This approach, although possibly costly, can get you out of a deadlocked situation and get the process going again.

# P A R T

# VI

# Arriving At Consensusville

## Successful Journey Checklist

☑ **Increased Level of Commitment**

☑ **Higher Level of Trust**

☑ **More Frequent and Open Communications**

☑ **Making Progress Toward Your Goals**

☑ **Fun!**

# WHERE YOU START YOUR JOURNEY IS NOT WHERE YOU END

*"When you walk what you talk . . . people listen."*

—Anonymous

No one wants to invest energy in something only to discover that no progress has been made. This is particularly true in the consensus process. However, the consensus process is one of the great methods for bringing people together to experience success. Some of the positive things you can look forward to in your journey to consensus are:

---

### *Successful Journey Checklist*

☑ **Increased Level of Commitment**

☑ **Higher Level of Trust**

☑ **More Frequent and Open Communications**

☑ **Making Progress Toward Your Goals**

☑ **Fun!**

---

## Increased Level of Commitment

Working to consensus requires more from you and the group than other methods. With consensus there should be no place to hide. Everyone should be giving much more compared to the old method of "just do what you are told." The wonderful thing about this new level of commitment is that as one person gives more, so too does the next person. The expectation and actions are that of growth rather than avoidance. This increased level of commitment and performance makes being part of the group a wonderful growing experience.

# WHERE YOU START YOUR JOURNEY IS NOT WHERE YOU END (continued)

## Higher Level of Trust

Trust can be slow to develop and easy to lose, but once a group has it in place, it's worth holding onto with great might. Trust can be maintained through a few key behaviors. Some of these we have already mentioned, but this is important enough to say again:

► Be honest. Say what's on your mind and be sure to say what you'll do and do what you say.

► Don't engage in hallway chatter about your group members. If an issue must be discussed, do it in your meeting. Backbiting is one of the great destroyers of trust.

► Trust the other people in your group. Trust is a two-way street.

► Give people the benefit of the doubt. If you are going to jump to a conclusion, why make it a negative one? People make mistakes and they aren't all directed at you. Ask questions to understand when things don't appear as they should. Invest in everyone's success.

As you and your group journey toward your goal using the consensus process, your trust levels will increase. Friendships will grow. Camaraderie will develop. You look forward to working with the people in your group and they look forward to seeing you.

## More Frequent and Open Communications

People like to be heard. It is a great compliment to have someone interested in what you have to say. Open communication is more than everyone having the chance to talk. It is being heard. It is feeling that the other person understands what you say. You can't overcommunicate with your group members. If there are major differences of opinion, probably not all information is on the table. Take responsibility for your communication. It is up to you to make sure that people get your message. Check for understanding frequently and clear up misunderstandings quickly. The sharing of information is a gift that should be acknowledged and valued by everyone in the group. As commitment and trust are established, communication becomes easier. You look forward to discussing options and working out issues together.

## Making Progress Toward Your Goals

One of the great joys in the consensus process is when goals get completed. Because there is such a high level of ownership, there is a higher level of personal satisfaction in making progress. You can enhance this feeling by celebrating the milestones as they are accomplished and designing goals that emphasize teamwork and results. Nothing is more powerful than a group of people who accomplish goals they set for themselves.

## Fun!

If you're not having any, then do it differently. With commitment, trust, open communication and progress, you should be having fun. The level of laughter is one of the measurement tools for this part of the process.

# WALKING THE TALK

You can be a role model and an advocate for working to consensus. You can make a difference in your next meeting, whether you are the leader or not. You have read the theory of consensus. You have taken stock of your personal skills. You have an understanding of the phases of mix, melt and mold. You have tools in your tool kit that will help you overcome obstacles in your way.

Now, apply some of this knowledge in your daily life. Test what works for you. Try different approaches. Maybe your next meeting will not change the course of the world, but it could make a difference to you and those around you. You can make a difference.

How many times have you been in meetings or situations that you considered to be a waste of time and wished that someone who knew what they were doing would *speak up and get things going?* **You can be that person!**

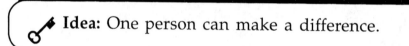

**Idea:** One person can make a difference.

By bringing the information in this book together with your group—you will be a Consensus Master leading the way to Consensusville.

> *One last question . . .*
> *Are you willing to be that person?*

# NOTES

# NOTES

# NOTES

# NOTES

# NOTES

# NOTES

# Now Available From

**THOMSON** ™

**NETg**

## Books•Videos•CD-ROMs•Computer-Based Training Products

## Subject Areas Include:

*Management*
*Human Resources*
*Communication Skills*
*Personal Development*
*Sales/Marketing*
*Finance*
*Coaching and Mentoring*
*Customer Service/Quality*
*Small Business and Entrepreneurship*
*Training*
*Life Planning*
*Writing*